GLASGOW
PAST & PRESENT

Ingram Street, from Candleriggs, *c.* 1946. (*ML*)

GLASGOW
PAST & PRESENT

BRUCE DURIE

First published in the United Kingdom in 2001 by
Sutton Publishing Limited exclusively for
WHSmith, Greenbridge Road, Swindon SN3 3LD

British Library Cataloguing in Publication Data
A catalogue record for this book is available from the British Library.

ISBN 0-7509-2846-8

Illustrations

Front endpaper: Anderston Cross railway and tram stations, *c.* 1910. (*ML*)
Back endpaper: Jamaica Bridge, 1925. (*ML*)
Half-title page: a Valentines postcard of the Bible Training Institute, 1905. The institute has been relocated and is now the International Christian College at the top of Byres Road. (*BD*)
Title page: a stroll across the canal at Spiers Wharf, Port Dundas, in 1955, looking south towards Payne Street and Colinton Street. (*ML*)

Typeset in 11/14pt Photina and produced by
Sutton Publishing Limited, Phoenix Mill,
Thrupp, Stroud, Gloucestershire GL5 2BU.
Printed and bound in England by
J.H. Haynes & Co. Ltd, Sparkford.

The Art Gallery's interior in 1927. (*BD*)

Contents

Two photographs of the back land at 492–492a Argyle Street, in 1919 and 1958 (*ML*). Latterly, this two-storey stone house (with a third storey of brick added) was the premises of John Cameron, general ironfounder.

The same block in Argyle Street (nos 470–504) in 1959 (*ML*), and (*right*) the Anderston Centre car park (*CP*).

Introduction

GLASGOW – WHAT CAN YOU SAY?

The twentieth century was both kind and cruel to Scotland's largest city, but no more so than any other century. However, few cities have had, and held on to, such national and international prominence for so long. In 1900 Glasgow was 'the second city of the Empire' with enlightened political stuctures and social amenities that were the envy of Victorian creations like Leeds and Birmingham. Municipal leaders came from cities abroad to see how it was done. Dominance in trade and industry were matched and balanced by renown in learning, the Arts, design and medicine. Commercial muscle was married to a cool head and a proud heart. If Edinburgh was the Athens of the North, Glasgow was more like a city-state in its organisation. And the River Clyde linked the 'dear green place' (*glas cu*) of St Mungo to every part of the map which was pink, and a lot more which wasn't.

Glasgow has an enviably long history. Early stone age fishing communities were replaced by a Celtic-Pictish culture and the local Dumnonii tribe traded peaceably with the Romans when they arrived at the settlement called Cathures around AD 80. The Romans built two great walls in Britain – Hadrian's Wall has its northern counterpart in the Antonine Wall which ran from what is now Old Kilpatrick, near Dumbarton, to Bridgeness in Fife, and marked the extreme north-western boundary of the Roman Empire.

In the fifth century Rome left, but Christianity stayed. Ireland and the west of Scotland were an important axis for the early Church and St Ninian consecrated a burial ground here when he visited in AD 380. Two centuries later St Mungo (St Kentigern) and his mother St Enoch (St Thenew or Thenog) built the first Episcopal church. Glaswegians choose to ignore the uncomfortable fact that their two patron saints came from Culross in Fife, on the other side of Scotland, in what is still regarded as the effete east!

Glasgow had been an important centre for the Church since 1115, and a burgh charter of 1180 recognised its status and provided for a new economy founded on commerce. Bishops and archbishops built the cathedral (consecrated in 1197) and, later, the university. James II gave a further charter to the bishop in 1450, 'erecting all his patrimony into a regality' – Glasgow was now effectively a royal burgh, with a population of 2,000 souls. The university was established the following year, making it the fourth oldest in the UK (after Oxford, Cambridge and St Andrews). The first archbishop, Robert Blacadder (1492), established a firm but short-lived episcopal grip which ended with the Reformation and the flight to Paris in 1560 of Glasgow's last Roman Catholic archbishop, James Beaton. He took many of the cathedral's records and relics but left a long-standing suspicion of Church power. Favourites of the tragic Mary Queen of Scots, Beaton and his

This postcard from 1907 shows the cathedral and the Royal Infirmary beside it. (*BD*)

two nephews, George Durie (Abbot of Dunfermline) and Andrew Durie (Abbot of Tongland and Bishop of Galloway), had long influenced Scottish politics.

But Beaton's exile left a power vacuum that was soon filled by greater civic power, wielded by emerging merchant and craft classes. In 1689 Glasgow ceased to be a 'Bishops Burgh'. The city, which had been unkindly (but not too unfairly) called a market village with a cathedral, started to become the 'merchant city'. The population had risen to 4,000 by 1550, 7,000 by 1600, and would double by 1660 to make it Scotland's second largest burgh; it exceeded 75,000 in the 1800s. Glasgow capitalised on its new maritime links and by the mid-1600s tobacco was being imported, laying a solid foundation for commercial affluence.

When Cromwell came to Glasgow in 1650, he saw the city's potential as a trading centre but realised it was held in check and 'kept under by the shallowness of the river'. Although a charter of 1490 had permitted the export of smoked and cured salmon, herring and other fish to Europe, Glasgow was not well-placed for European trade and unfair English protectionism in the shape of the Navigation Laws had denied Glasgow the ability to trade with the tobacco and sugar planters in the New World – although the city's merchants didn't scorn the odd bit of smuggling to get round the restrictions. However, the 1707 Union of the Crowns allowed expansion into the lucrative American trade which led to many firm links and much interchange. American independence in 1776 threatened this, but it was gradually strengthened by the transportation and voluntary emigration of Scots over the next two centuries. In any case, most of Glasgow's trading links were with the West Indies rather than with North America.

The same view as that on page 12 but taken more recently shows the degree of redevelopment in this area over the last century. High-rise housing and new roads have appeared, although many of Glasgow's historic buildings have survived more or less intact or at least sympathetically modernised. (*CP*)

The long-standing problem of the River Clyde's shallowness was finally addressed by 1770. By flushing the silt from the river bed via jetties along the banks, it became more readily navigable. Port Glasgow, towards the mouth of the Clyde, had cemented the Atlantic trade and by the mid-1770s sizeable ships could sail right into the city centre. With growing maritime traffic which needed to be dispersed inland, Glasgow became an important transport centre. Coaches and flys left for all parts of Scotland from Thomas Durie's Black Bull Inn in Argyle Street.

The Forth & Clyde Canal, connecting Glasgow to Edinburgh, was the world's first manmade sea-to-sea ship canal, linking the Atlantic Ocean to what was then called the 'German Ocean' (the North Sea). Such a link was first suggested during the reign of Charles II, primarily as a passage for warships, but it took a hundred years to come to anything. Several surveys in the early eighteenth century attracted the support of, *inter alia*, Daniel Defoe and the Scots architect William Adam. Unusually, the estimated costs for building the canal went down rather than up – the late seventeenth-century estimate of £500,000 dropped to £80,000 in 1760. Three years later the Board of Trustees for the Encouragement of Fisheries, Manufactures & Improvements in Scotland appointed the Yorkshire engineer John Smeaton to survey the route. At this time the Clyde was only 4 ft deep in Glasgow, so bringing the canal into the city centre would limit the river's usefulness. Smeaton's proposals (to bypass the city) outraged the Glasgow tobacco merchants who commissioned a rival survey, from Robert Mackell and James Watt, local

The Royal Infirmary and the cathedral alongside. (*CP*)

boy made good. Edinburgh dismissed the Glasgow counter-proposals as 'a ditch, a gutter, a mere puddle' which would do nothing for 'magnificence and national honour'.

The proponents of a 'grand canal' won and Smeaton revised his plans. The canal was 35 miles long, with an additional 3.5 miles on the branch into Port Dundas. It was 60 ft wide and 9 ft deep, rose to 156 ft above sea level and went through 20 locks on the eastern side and 19 on the western. The Kelvin Aqueduct built to carry it was the largest of its kind in Britain and the area behind it became known as Butney, after Botany Bay, because of the convict labour used. It opened in July 1790 but gave way to the railway in 1867.

If the railways sounded the canal's death knell, road transport delivered the killing blow. In 1948 it was taken over by the British Transport Commission and in 1962 by the British Waterways Board. All rights to navigation ceased on 1 January 1963 when it was decided to close the canal rather than invest £160,000 in building a lift-bridge at the Denny bypass on the Glasgow–Stirling road. However, the £78m Millennium Link project has since restored the Forth & Clyde and Union Canals to their former glory, making them fully navigable for the first time in almost forty years.

Meanwhile, back in the eighteenth century, the industrial revolution was taking Glasgow along a new but natural path into engineering, steel making and shipbuilding, making the best of the Scottish practical temperament. This drove the city's development for the next hundred years or more. Industrialists and merchants were by then into cotton and other

Today, the cathedral precinct is pedestrianised. (*CP*)

textiles, and the manufacture of paper, glass, sugar and soap, plus distilling, bleaching, dyeing and textile printing, merged into a well-founded chemical industry. Cotton alone, at its height, employed over 30 per cent of the Glasgow workforce. The American Civil War in 1861 and increasing competition from Manchester and other newly industrial cities could have strangled Glasgow's economy, but shipbuilding, steam locomotive construction and other engineering started since iron ore and coal were in ready supply and near to hand. This provided the economic backdrop to a revolutionary period in art and design. Charles Rennie Mackintosh, Alexander ('Greek') Thomson and others framed the city's commercial and industrial prosperity in golden light. And while Scottish soldiers were fighting to keep the map pink everywhere, their civilian cousins were providing the empire with railways, bridges, canals and telegraphs. When Queen Victoria came to the throne, she had more or less the same communications technology as Julius Caesar had known. When she died in 1901, Scottish ingenuity had provided road, rail and radio. Glasgow played no small part in these and other innovations, as the names MacAdam, Watt and Baird testify.

From 1900 life was hard for many, but there was work in factories, foundries, shipyards, mills and shops. New workers came from the rest of Scotland, from Ireland (many of them descendants of Scots transplanted there in earlier centuries) and from the rest of the empire. There was also a large influx of Jewish and Italian immigrants – the latter leaving a lasting mark in the various cafés, ice-cream businesses and delicatessens. The city assimilated nearby villages and communities – Anderston, Bridgeton, Calton, the Gorbals, Kelvingrove and Woodside in 1846; Govanhill, Hillhead, Kelvinside, Maryhill and Pollokshields in 1891; and Cathcart, Govan, Partick and Pollokshaws in 1912. It became, and remains, Scotland's largest city and Britain's third largest regional centre.

And of course, 'Clyde-built' vessels were world-famous. The great cargo ships, passenger liners and warships were the proud products of Glasgow, symbols of its sturdy worth. But this period also saw the building of tenement slums where people were more or less abandoned to their fates. When the postwar 1920s led to the depression of the 1930s the poor living conditions worsened. The Glasgow of the 1940s had a million inhabitants, many of them badly housed and inadequately fed. The Second World War provided a brief burst of prosperity but the period after it was marked by the growth of soulless housing estates and the removal of literally hundreds of thousands of people to new towns like Cumbernauld, East Kilbride and Irvine. Many of the younger ones felt divested of hope and opportunity and saw better prospects in Canada, America, New Zealand, Australia and South Africa.

Fifty years on and the large industries of the past are gone, taking with them many of the small businesses that supplied and were sustained by them. But there is new heart. Edinburgh has the Scottish Parliament, but Glasgow is home to many branches of its executive arm. Education, financial services, telecommunications, the media, software, tourism and light industry have found a home there and shipbuilding is once again on the agenda. The many museums, galleries, world-famous art collections and well-maintained historic buildings sit happily alongside new landmark architecture, many a multinational headquarters and two additional universities. When Glasgow took the titles European City of Culture (1990) and City of Architecture and Design (1999) from under Edinburgh's nose it provided a much-needed fillip and a validation of Glaswegians' sense of self-worth.

True, the relaxation of the arcane licensing laws in 1976 helped to alleviate much of the drunkenness and resultant social problems that fermented in rough pubs and removed the need to get 'swalley'd up' before the 10 p.m. closing time and not at all on a Sunday, except illegally. Now elegant café bars make for more tranquil enjoyment. Glasgow claims, with some justification, the most vivacious nightlife and the best shopping in the UK outside London. And if the smaller shops have been replaced by designer malls of glass and chrome, these are at least the equal of any in the world.

The new building on the Clyde – the SECC, the £75m complex of Science Centre, Glasgow Tower and Imax Theatre – and the redevelopment of much of the city centre mirrors a new inner pride. The 'dear green place' is bisected by motorways, but no one doubts the city would become one big traffic jam without them. Glasgow is a 'merchant city' once again, a City of Culture, a field of dreams. As the slogan goes, 'Glasgow's Miles Better'. Than what, they don't say. But who cares?

No mean city? I raised this grim spectre with a local while researching this book. He pointed out that 'mean' in that sense indicates 'average'. 'And we're never that, son, never that!'

The City Centre

Bath Street, Anderston, looking west from the Pitt Street intersection towards St Matthew's Blythswood parish church, 1964. (*ML*)

Nos 106–160 Pitt Street, Anderston, at the corner of Bothwell Street, 1959. (*ML*)

Pitt Street now. The photograph on the left (*CP*) shows roughly the same view as that above, although the structure of the intersection has changed. On the right is another view along Pitt Street. The church is now a nightclub and further along are the Scottish Enterprise building in Bothwell Street, the Novotel and the Strathclyde police headquarters (*CP*).

(*Above, left*): Argyle Street is closer to the hearts of true Glaswegians than the more famous Sauchiehall Street. It has seen many changes. This postcard is franked 1907, but is from an earlier picture (*BD*). (*Above, right*): Argyle Street today, taken from Central station (*CP*).

Day and night in Argyle Street, 1962. (*Left*): 186–154 Argyle Street (*ML*); (*bottom left*): the junction with Union Street, east of Central station (*ML*). The 2001 view (*bottom right*) shows the superimposition of newer retailers, notably KFC and Waterstones, and the predominance of youth culture (*CP*).

Lawson's clothing and furniture shop at 363 Argyle Street on the corner of James Watt Street in 1900 (*ML*). The lower photograph shows the same building more recently, with the Café l'Etoile on the ground floor (*CP*).

Central station and the Station Hotel have also changed markedly, not least in the surroundings, as this 1907 drawing (*BD*) and the accompanying modern shots (*CP*) illustrate. However, the basic structure of the hotel and the famous station canopy remain intact.

Anderston is now a bustling commercial and industrial sector with many government offices. Contrast this 1909 postcard view (*BD*) with the 1970s pictures opposite and the equivalent view today, shown left (*CP*). The tall structure is the titanium-clad tower at Pacific Quay.

(*Right*): Anderston Cross bus station in
1972 (*ML*) and (*below*) the Anderston
industrial estate (*ML*) in 1978.

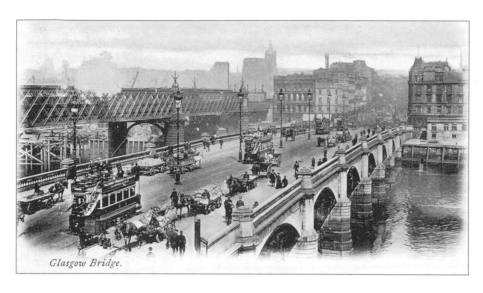

Glasgow Bridge.

Leading to Central station and
Anderston is Jamaica Bridge,
pictured here in two postcards
from 1902 and 1912 (*BD*), and
in 2001 (*CP*).

Jamaica Street, leading to the bridge, has long been an important thoroughfare, and its name reflects the previous dependence on trade with the West Indies. These 1890s (*ML*) and 1914 (*ML*) pictures show the new fangled motor lorries and electric trolley-buses in a bustling street.

Now Jamaica Street is bleak and uninviting. Wetherspoon's pub/café on the right is the only building on the street that looks cared for. (*CP*)

Charing Cross seen from the west along Sauchiehall Street in 1926 (*ML*); seen from Newton Place (*left*) the influence of modern traffic systems is all too clear (*CP*).

Charing Cross Mansions now houses a cosmopolitan array of businesses from Starbucks coffee shop to a Mexican bar-restaurant (*CP*). And where Charing Cross itself once stood, a motorway now takes traffic east and west. The Mitchell Library still stands. (*CP*)

Once-grand Victorian architecture has given way to this controversial building with its bridge that goes nowhere (*CP*). St George's Mansions is now framed by motorway access roads (*CP*).

Sauchiehall Street has also seen its share of changes. These two views, looking east from Charing Cross, date from 1895 (*ML*) and 1900 (*BD*).

(*Below*): two modern views of Sauchiehall Street. (*Left*): the view looking west towards Charing Cross; (*right*): the pedestrian precinct from the Concert Hall and Buchanan Galleries, further east. (*CP*)

By the 1970s Sauchiehall Street had taken the shape and nature it has today, with new buildings and redevelopment. These three photographs are the view looking east from the McLellan Galleries in the 1970s (*ML*); at Trerons (*ML*); and the view from the McLellan Galleries looking east in 2001, taken from roughly where the bus is in the middle photograph (*CP*). Work to improve traffic flow and pedestrian access is continual. The white building on the right-hand side is the Willow Tea-rooms, a shrine to Charles Rennie Mackintosh and the benefits of a nice cuppa.

(*Above and right*): these two postcard
views of Buchanan Street, *c.* 1900
and 1934 (*BD*), show the steadily
encroaching influence of both the
motor car and retail consumerism.
(*Below*): the modern-day view from
the same vantage point (*CP*).

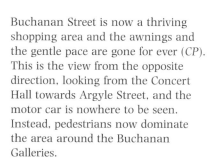

Buchanan Street in 1964, shown here looking north from Argyle Street. (*ML*)

Buchanan Street is now a thriving shopping area and the awnings and the gentle pace are gone for ever (*CP*). This is the view from the opposite direction, looking from the Concert Hall towards Argyle Street, and the motor car is nowhere to be seen. Instead, pedestrians now dominate the area around the Buchanan Galleries.

Many streets have been swept
away or changed irretrievably
by the Clydeside Expressway.
McIntyre Street, pictured above
in 1930 (*ML*), is a good example
of the many changes to
Anderston and the area towards
the West End.

McIntyre Street is still
residential, but is now different
in character. The trees obscure
the Clydeside Expressway off-
ramp behind no. 18. (*CP*)

Woodlands Road has also seen dramatic changes. It is shown here in 1958, looking towards Charing Cross from the junction with St George's Road (*ML*). Trams and trolley-buses once trundled along quiet roads where now the M8 roars past, just beyond the corner in thc lowcr picture (*CP*).

To the east of the city centre, the Saltmarket joins Albert Bridge to Trongate and the Cross. This 1868 crowd, gathered specially for the camera (but unable to stand still long enough!) is looking south away from Bridgegate. (*ML*)

These two photographs, taken looking north up the Saltmarket towards Glasgow Cross and the Tolbooth, date from *c.* 1904 and 1958. (*ML*)

This is Trongate in 1774, looking east from Candleriggs, from a drawing by James Brown (*ML*), and the equivalent view of the Trongate today (*CP*).

Three views of the Trongate and Tron
Steeple. The top photograph looks west
from Glasgow Cross, and the second
faces east along Trongate; both these
pictures date from around 1909 (*BD*).
The modern picture below is taken
from the Saltmarket (*CP*).

Tontine House and the Tolbooth at the Trongate around 1890 and 1930 (*ML*), and below in 2001 (*CP*). The Tolbooth has always been a source of annoyance to city traffic planners, but it still stands in splendid isolation, in defiance of their attempts to remove it.

These three contemporary photographs show the view from Candleriggs to Bell Street, with the Merchant Square development and new flats; the view down Wilson Street where it intersects with Candleriggs; and the view along Candleriggs from the same viewpoint. They show clearly that redevelopment has been patchy, and much remains to be done. (*CP*)

The early postcard view (*BD*) and the modern shot below (*CP*) show Renfield Street to be remarkably unchanged above the new shop fronts on the ground floor. The famous electric trolley-buses are still missed, but they are impractical in modern Glasgow.

These two postcard views (*opposite*) of George Square (*BD*) date from just after the turn of the twentieth century. The electric trams and the motorcar were already making their influence felt. Pictures taken recently show the layout of the square to be basically unchanged, but advertising is less subtle. The hoarding covers a building under redevelopment as an art gallery in 2001 (*CP*).

41

Modern buildings abound in the area around Renfrew Street and Cowcaddens. Clockwise from top left are: the Scottish Media Group headquarters at Cowcaddens; the Scottish Ambulance Service headquarters in Maitland Street; the view from Renfrew Street from the Hope Street post office, showing the UGC Cinema next to the ancient Pavilion, opposite Scottish Television, and further along, the Concert Hall and the new John Lewis building; and the Royal Scottish Academy of Music and Drama. (CP)

Some of the older buildings in the area have been tastefully redeveloped. The upper photograph is of the Piping Centre in Maitland Street, brought to its new use in 1995–97. (*Below*): the Theatre Royal in Renfrew Street. (*CP*)

(*Above, left*): the old Royal Exchange building shown in this 1908 postcard (*BD*) is now the centre of an upmarket shopping, restaurant and designer-label quarter. (*Above, right*): note the artistically positioned traffic cone on the statue outside what is now the art gallery. The building behind the old Exchange is now Borders bookshop and café (*CP*).

The primary school at 210 Kent Road, Anderston, pictured here in 1964 before its demolition, was designed by W. Landless (1885–6) and built in 1886 (*ML*). The new architecture is soulless by comparison. The new school is behind this bungalow, which is today's no. 210 (*CP*).

The River Clyde –
The City's Heartblood

Today, the River Clyde is more to do with what happens on its banks than the river itself. The Moat House Hotel is an example of such development. (*CP*)

The industry on the river needed coal for power. Coal was also exported via the Clyde. These coal barges are on the Forth & Clyde Canal at North Spiers Wharf, Craighall Road, in about 1900 (*ML*). (*Below left*): the view across the canal from Craighall Road (*CP*). (*Below right*): this is the view from the wharf towards Payne Street, looking towards what is now the motorway, with the Port Dundas Trading Estate to the left (*CP*).

Spiers Wharf, Port Dundas, in 1955 (*ML*). (*Below*): the wharf today looks desolate and uncared for (*CP*).

Glasgow imported raw materials and exported finished products all over the world, but was primarily concerned with the Atlantic trade. In the nineteenth century Kingston Dock was a major berth for sailing ships. (*ML*)

However, trade was where you found it. These two 1926 photographs show the Clydevilla crane loading the SS *Belfri* with locomotives for the Egyptian State Railways. (*ML*)

Today, there is trade of a different kind at the Broomielaw, as these modern pictures of the Moat House and Hilton hotels show. (*CP*)

The famous 175-ton Finnieston crane loaded many of the ships. It also dominated the skyline (and still does) and afforded stunning views along the river. These photographs, both taken from the Finnieston crane just after the Second World War, show (*left*) the view eastwards along Lancefield Quay and Anderston Quay and (*below*) Stobcross Quay and Queen's Dock. (*ML*)

The Finnieston crane remains a major feature of the Clyde, but many other characteristics are largely gone. These two contemporary pictures show (*right*) Bell's Bridge from the Moat House Hotel and (*below*) the view eastwards along Finnieston and Lancefield Quays from Bell's Bridge to Kingston Bridge and the Southern Rotunda. (*CP*)

The River Clyde was also a travel route – both on it and under it. The Harbour Tunnel rotunda is shown here taking horse-drawn traffic from Finnieston in 1896. (*ML*)

(*Right*): there was considerable commuter traffic, and the pleasure-boating market was also buoyant as Glaswegians travelled 'doon the watter'. (*Below*): the *May Queen* leaving her berth. (*ML*)

In contrast to the jolly 1900 postcard of a cruise from the Broomielaw (*BD*), the *Pride of Clyde*, moored under Glasgow Bridge, looks rather forlorn (*CP*).

But if Glasgow's dependence on shipping has necessarily diminished from the busy times shown above, with vessels leaving King George V Dock in the 1960s (*ML*), there is a new optimism in the Science Centre complex, the SECC, and the many companies whose offices are strung along the Broomielaw and in Anderston (*CP*).

The North

The premises of W.B. Milne, stationer, newsagent and tobacconist, at
329 Springburn Road, Springburn, 1900. (*ML*)

Maryhill, some 3 miles north-west of the city centre, was established by Robert Graham in the late 1700s and named after his wife, Mary Hill. Locals would laugh to realise that the first Temperance society in Britain was founded here when Graham's daughter Lilias became teetotal in 1829. By then, Maryhill was an industrial community – making paper, textiles, lumber, iron and boats. A police burgh since 1856, it was annexed by Glasgow in 1912. Charles Rennie Mackintosh designed Queens Cross Church in 1899. It is now the headquarters of the Charles Rennie Mackintosh Society. These two pictures show Maryhill's other famous institution, the Army Barracks (now no more) with the Scots Greys on parade around 1900 (*ML*). The comparison picture below is from the 1960s (*ML*).

Bairds Brae in Maryhill, showing the old houses on the canal beside Oakbank Hospital in 1955 (*ML*). The modern picture shows the new headquarters of British Waterways Scotland, and the canal is finding new life (*CP*).

Springburn, to the north of the city, grew with the railways and declined with them, too. At its peak, Springburn was Britain's major railway centre – over 8,000 people were employed in building locomotives here for export to over sixty countries. But the companies failed to move with the times, in particular the arrival of diesel and electric trains. The North British Locomotive Company closed first, followed by the rest over the next twenty years, until locomotives were no longer part of the industrial base of Springburn. The last works, St Rollox, closed in 1988. Tenement demolition has left Springburn short of housing and most of the population moved to the high-rise flats in nearby Balornock. New housing, as shown here, dominates (CP). In nearby Sighthill cemetery is a monument to John Baird and Andrew Hardie, who were involved in the so-called Radical Rising of 1820.

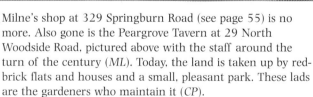

Milne's shop at 329 Springburn Road (see page 55) is no more. Also gone is the Peargrove Tavern at 29 North Woodside Road, pictured above with the staff around the turn of the century (ML). Today, the land is taken up by red-brick flats and houses and a small, pleasant park. These lads are the gardeners who maintain it (CP).

Three contrasting pictures of a pub at 1512
Maryhill Road. The old Art Nouveau
frontage shown above in 1937 (*ML*)
contrasts with the new look (*right*) in 1939
(*ML*). Now it's The Botany, named not as
any reference to parks and gardens, but
because the locks on the Forth & Clyde Canal
nearby were called the Botany (or Butney)
Locks. Convicted criminals were given the
choice between working on building the
canal or transportation to Botany Bay,
Australia (*CP*).

In 1936 Possil was justly proud of its new shops at 132–146 Balmore Road (*ML*) and this confectioner's shop at 19 Barloch Street, Possilpark, brand-new in 1934. (*ML*)

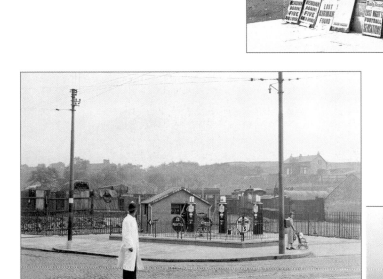

(*Above*): a traffic policeman on duty by the filling station at 2 Saracen Street, Possilpark, in 1934; this would be a rare sight today (*ML*). (*Right*): Miltonbank Primary School in Scalpay Street, pictured here in 1970, is more typical of Possil's current architecture (*ML*).

The East

Red Road flats, Balornock, in the 1980s. (*ML*)

Compare this photograph with the one on the previous page. This is the same view of Red Road, looking north, in 1925, before development. Easterhouse, just north of the M8 motorway, was typical of these tower-block developments. It was acquired by Glasgow from Lanarkshire in 1938 for residential housing. The first peripheral housing estate was started in 1954 but without any planning for shops or recreational amenities. Nor was there much by way of local employment. As a result, the area became a by-word for poor planning and poorer people. Since the 1980s, housing associations and private developers have tried to improve the area, with patchy and limited success.

(*Opposite*): Swinton Main Street, Baillieston, *c*. 1900 (*ML*). Baillieston, east of the city centre and north of the Clyde, was a mining town. Now largely residential, it was incorporated into Glasgow in 1975. Baker and pastry maker Robert Lauchlan had a shop in Main Street, Baillieston. As late as 1925 he was still using his horse cart for deliveries (*ML*).

Agriculture and industry sat side by side in the east of Glasgow. These men harvesting potatoes at Findlay's Nurseries, Springhill, in 1946 (*ML*) may well have been miners making extra income during the 'tattie-howking' season. If so, they probably worked at one of the many nearby pits, such as the Cadder (*ML*).

(*Left*): Mckinnon & Browning's premises and tenements, Carntyne, *c.* 1902.

(*Right*): Carntyne is now largely low-rise housing on wide boulevards like Carntynehall Road and industry is restricted to the Carmelon Road Estate. (*CP*)

This taxi-cab office and garage amid tenements at 11–29 Port Dundas Road, shown above in 1925 (*ML*), is now a landscaped site ready for redevelopment (*CP*).

Old villages such as Carntyne and Springhill are now bypassed. By 1971 the M8 had taken the congestion away from the city but it also altered many communities by planting its concrete legs where once there had been houses and shops. (*ML*)

Laying the memorial stone of Cowlairs parish church in Gourlay Street in 1899. The church is no longer there. (*ML*)

Munro Cleaners and other businesses at
109–113 New City Road, at the
junction with Scott Street in 1964 (*ML*).
Munro's is now an electrical appliance
store but looks largely unchanged.

The garage at Cowlairs Co-operative, Morrin Street, seen
here in 1934 (*ML*), also looks much the same in 2001 (*CP*).

Many of the great thoroughfares in and out of Glasgow have been supplanted by A-roads and motorways. This pub at 615 Great Eastern Road, Parkhead, enjoyed abundant passing trade in 1923 (*ML*). The Sheddens pub in the Shettleston Road remains, although customers and other street life are strangely absent (*CP*).

East Glasgow's other famous feature is the 'Bar-L', as Her Majesty's Prison at Barlinnie in Riddrie is usually known. This picture dates from 1955. (*ML*)

The South

Cathcart Castle, 1915. The castle is no more and the land on which it stood has been cleared for development.

The postcard above shows Maxwell Park in 1908 (*BD*); the view is almost unchanged today (*CP*). Pollokshields Burgh Hall is untouched, although the pond looks smaller and the houses are thankfully obscured by sympathetic tree planting. Pollokshields, on the city's south side, was originally two separate burghs, Pollokshields West and Pollokshields East. One developed shops and industry, but the feus of the other did not permit this. Both were incorporated into Glasgow in 1891 but retain their different characters. Pollok Country Park to the west houses the internationally famous Burrell Art Collection and Pollok golf course. Nearby is Haggs Castle (1585), now Glasgow's Museum of Childhood.

Cathcart is an ancient parish to the south of Glasgow. It was originally founded on agriculture and weaving, but later papermills grew up along the banks of the River Cart. The opening of the Cathcart District Railway in 1884 and easy travelling for commuters led to the development of tenements and more up-market villas. Cathcart became part of Glasgow proper in 1912. Glasgow's 'South-side' had much to recommend it – including the gentle pleasures of Rouken Glen, with its tea-rooms, boating lake and pavilion, as depicted in this Edwardian postcard. (*BD*)

Buchan & Tennant had a garage at 3 Station Road, Cathcart, in 1933 (*ML*). As ever, old buildings find new uses. This one, near Cathcart Bridge, is now a restaurant (*CP*).

For years the Gorbals was synonymous with poor housing and social deprivation. This back lane at 103–137 Coburg Street in 1912 is typical (*ML*). It is now partly redeveloped on one side, with a gap site on the other (*CP*).

Yet the Gorbals was not totally devoid
of amenities, and the general reading
room at the Main Street Library had
significant custom in 1907, especially
for the free newspapers. (*ML*)

And there was the Bedford Cinema at 117 Eglinton Street,
shown here in 1924 (*ML*) and 2001 (*CP*). The original
cinema was damaged by fire and the art deco New Bedford
was built in just nine months. Run as a cinema by Green's for
many years, it later became a bingo hall. Now, much the
worse for wear, it is closed.

Eglinton Toll, looking north up Pollokshaws Road. By 1917 there was an electricity generating station here, currently a printworks (*ML*). The toll is now occupied by the St Andrews Cross (*CP*). The rather splendid iron canopy shelter is a greatly missed feature.

Pollokshaws was and is very different from the Gorbals. Sitting on the White Cart Water south of the Clyde, it was originally a textile village and became a burgh of barony in 1813. It boasted Glasgow's first linen printworks in 1742, iron foundries, a gas-lit cotton mill and paper mills. It was famous for its working-class militancy, and the socialist MP James Maxton was born there. Redeveloped in the 1960s, Pollokshaws is now a mixture of old tenements and new flats.

Two famous old pubs, at the corner of Norfolk Street and Bridge Street, were open for business in 1933 (*ML*). Still going strong in a redeveloped guise is The Glaswegian (*CP*).

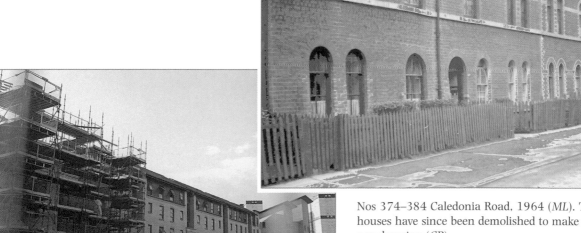

Nos 374–384 Caledonia Road, 1964 (*ML*). These houses have since been demolished to make way for new housing (*CP*).

By 1955 it was clear that slum housing like this in Florence Street and Cumberland Street, Hutchesontown, was no longer acceptable and a programme of new building was planned (*ML*). Now there are industrial units on one side of Cumberland Road and on the other side, at Gorbals Cross, newer high-rise flats (*CP*).

Castlemilk was one of the beneficiaries of the housing explosion of the 1960s. Shops like these at 5–9 Croftfoot Road were prevalent in the 1940s (*ML*). Takeaways are the new vogue (*CP*).

By 1962 the development of new corporation housing had started. These multi-storey flats at Dougrie Place, Castlemilk, were typical of the breed. They are shown under construction (*ML*) and in their finished state (*CP*).

By the 1970s it was obvious that high-rise flats with no supporting amenities were no longer a suitable way to house people (*ML*). Since then there have been many social programmes intended to alleviate these problems, leading to more sympathetic types of development, with mixed-tenure housing and business units. The complex in the lower right picture is housed in the property built on the grounds of the demolished Glenwood School. It was previously occupied by the Castlemilk Economic Development Agency, a ten-year government-funded project to address issues such as social exclusion and hopelessness (*CP*).

The Battlefield Monument and the Victoria Infirmary shown in the postcard above (*BD*) are largely still in place, but a new roundabout deals with the increased traffic. The church is no longer there (*CP*).

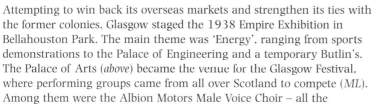

Attempting to win back its overseas markets and strengthen its ties with the former colonies, Glasgow staged the 1938 Empire Exhibition in Bellahouston Park. The main theme was 'Energy', ranging from sports demonstrations to the Palace of Engineering and a temporary Butlin's. The Palace of Arts (*above*) became the venue for the Glasgow Festival, where performing groups came from all over Scotland to compete (*ML*). Among them were the Albion Motors Male Voice Choir – all the choristers were on nightshift work so they rehearsed between 2 and 3 a.m.! Like its modern-day counterpart, the Millennium Dome in Greenwich, the Palace had disappointing attendance figures: only 12.5 million instead of the expected 20 million. The weather was blamed, as was the need to close the Palace on Sundays. The showpiece was the spectacular 300-ft-high Tait Tower (*above right*), a symbol of modernism (*ML*). Today, the site is marked only by a stone memorial and a plinth where the tower stood (*CP*).

The West

Byres Road, looking north from near Ashton Road, Hillhead, *c.* 1967. (*ML*)

Partick, often called 'Pertick' or 'Pertmet', was granted to the Bishop of Glasgow in 1136 by King David I. The name derives from *Perdeyc*, meaning 'small woodland'. The nearby River Kelvin provided power for the many watermills used in the eighteenth and nineteenth centuries to help make paper, silt-iron and flint. In the 1840s shipbuilding started on both sides of the River Kelvin and continued into the 1960s. Partick was a police burgh until incorporated into the city in 1912.

The famous F&F Ballroom at 201 Dumbarton Road, Partick, was at its height in 1940 (*ML*). It is now a bingo hall (*CP*).

St Mary's Old Masonic Bar at 165 Dumbarton Road, shown in this rather indistinct shot from about 1924 (*ML*), is now the Partick Tavern (*CP*).

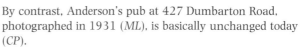

By contrast, Anderson's pub at 427 Dumbarton Road, photographed in 1931 (*ML*), is basically unchanged today (*CP*).

Nearby Partickhill was not short of amenities. The Partickhill Bowling and Tennis Club in Partickhill Avenue is pictured here in about 1905 (*ML*) and 2001 (*CP*).

Govan was Scotland's fifth largest burgh (established in 1862) before becoming part of Glasgow in 1912. Constantine built a religious centre here in the sixth century and was later buried there. The parish originally included the Gorbals (separated in the eighteenth century) and Partick. Many of Govan's older buildings and streets are gone, but some local traditions remain, such as the annual Govan Old Fair. The Govan Old Victualling Society is the UK's oldest co-operative society. Here we see Langlands Road and Shaw Street, Govan, around 1960 (*ML*). Today, the street is blocked off at the end of a residential area (*CP*).

(*Left*): Govan was always about shipbuilding. This picture was taken in Govan Road in 1883, from the corner of Carmichael Street, looking east (*ML*). (*Below*): now the view is dominated by the Science Centre, the titanium-clad Tower and Imax (*CP*).

(*Left*): the same area in 1912 shows Fairfields shipyard from the river (*ML*). In the mid-nineteenth century shipbuilding became a mainstay of the local economy, raising the population but creating an over-dependence on the industry. Today there is only one shipyard left.

(*Right*): the present-day view, taken from the end of Govan Road looking over to the Clyde Port Authority, shows how the purpose and nature of the river has changed with the move away from dependence on shipbuilding. (*CP*)

In 1910 the Acme Tea Chest Co. at 204 Polmadie Road, Govanhill Street, was a smoke nuisance and contributed significantly to local pollution (*ML*). Acme site survives, occupied by more hi-tech businesses, and is now altogether more pleasant to look at and a lot less polluting (*CP*).

By the early nineteenth century Meikle Govan (so-called to distinguish it from Little Govan or the Gorbals) had developed from a small village into a centre of coal-mining. This was made possible by the deepening of the River Clyde. Other industries also sprang up to take advantage of the nearby coal. This 1931 view (*ML*) of Queen's Park Works at 287 Aikenhead Road, Govanhill, contrasts with the present-day Alcan Foil Europe building (*CP*).

The Western Infirmary in Byres Road, from Partick Bridge, outside the Kelvin Hall, 1906 (*ML*). The same view today (*left*) is obscured by trees (*CP*). Alongside it stands the new infirmary extension, shown below (*CP*).

The Western Infirmary and its neighbour Glasgow University have long been the twin pillars of the city's international renown in medicine. This 1904 postcard presents a view not very different from that of today (*BD*). Both retain much of their original Victorian character.

Other parts of Kelvingrove have perhaps fared less well, as a comparison of this 1925 postcard (*BD*) and the modern equivalent (*CP*) shows.

In 1955 bowling was permitted in Kelvingrove Park (*ML*). Now, the bowling area is a car park and the view towards the university is obscured by trees (*CP*). But at least the children have some amenities (*CP*).

Glasgow's renowned physicist Lord Kelvin still sits in the park whose name he took when ennobled (*CP*), but the trees have grown somewhat since the 1916 postcard shown above left (*BD*).

The University's Old College Gateway has remained virtually unchanged from this 1904 postcard view (*BD*) to the present day (*CP*).

The same cannot be said of Great Western Road where it meets Byres Road. The trams are gone, as are the lamp-posts that stood in the centre of the road in 1902 (*BD*). The entrance to the Botanic Gardens looks much the same (*CP*).

In the Palm House in the Botanic Gardens non-smoking was the rule, even in 1904 – and nae chuckin' yir dowps in the pond, neither! (*BD*). Anyway, it's just a big plant-pot nowadays. The palm tree is under threat of removal (*CP*).

The justly famous Art Gallery has seen much of its gardens give way to roads, as shown in the 1933 postcard (*BD*) and the modern picture shown below left (*CP*). One of the Gallery's claims to fame is that it is built back-to-front, as the photograph of the back (which should have been the front entrance) clearly shows (*CP*). It is said that the builders got the plans upside down and when the architect saw the foundations laid the wrong way round, he killed himself in despair.

The Kelvin Hall, as depicted on a 1940 postcard (but from an earlier picture) (*BD*). It is basically unchanged today, apart from the concessions to the motor car (*CP*).

Some 5 miles north-west of the city centre lies Drumchapel. The land here was bought by Glasgow Corporation in 1939 in order to build a housing estate but the war intervened, putting the project back almost ten years. 'The Drum' as it is known housed more than 30,000 people, but with all-too-common lack of foresight it was short of amenities, services and job opportunities. It became synonymous with unemployment, poverty, vandalism and other social problems. The war memorial is still there, as is St Andrew's & St Mary's parish church at 122 Drumchapel Road, pictured in 1922 (*ML*), and looking even better today (*CP*).

The middle-class semi-rural housing built in this area, like these semi-detached bungalows at 158–160 Golf Drive pictured in 1938 (*ML*), remains basically unchanged today, albeit the residents now have the benefit of UPVC windows and the telephone (*CP*).

Knightswood is another area that has changed out of all recognition; compare this 1925 view of Knightswood Road (*ML*) with one from the present day (*CP*). Now it connects Anniesland to the sweep of the Great Western Road.

Closer into the centre, the elegant houses surrounding Victoria Park were far enough away from the rest of riverside Whiteinch for middle-class comfort. Victoria Park Drive South in 1910, with the only traffic a horse and trap (*ML*), is a far cry from the present scene (*CP*).

We Arra Peepel!

Glasgow is really all about its people, not its high-rise blocks, slum tenements and new shopping arcades. A case in point is the 'clippies', the tram and bus conductresses, who were loved, hated, respected and feared in equal measure. Their famous battle-cries such as 'If hauf o' yiz got aff there'd be room for all o' yiz' struck terror into the strongest heart. These two are showing off their new uniforms in 1939, when female employment started to rise as the men went to war. (*ML*)

Matheson's boot repair shop at 418 Argyle Street was typical of the businesses which abounded in the area in the early years of the twentieth century (*ML*). It is hard to see how anyone would get a heel fixed at the same location today, unless they asked the Scottish Executive, now at no. 450, for a grant! (*CP*)

There are lots of ways to make a few bob! Breaking sticks, like the children in this courtyard around 1910, is one way. (*ML*)

Busking for the punters near Nelson Mandela Place eighty years later is another. (*CP*)

Glaswegians have always made their own sporting entertainment, whether in amateur football teams like the Linthouse Football Club, Govan, in 1887–8 (*ML*) or in the gentler but no less vicious game of curling. (*Below*): members of the Partick Curling Club, Dumbarton (10th) Province, enjoying their Bonspiel at Loch Ardinning, possibly in 1932 (*ML*).

Housing for the people has improved immensely since this group of women and children were photographed at 118 High Street in 1868. (*ML*)

By the 1920s conditions were not much better, but at least they got the washing done. This slum housing at 83 Nelson Street is long gone. (*ML*)

Often, the city-centre housing has been replaced by more utilitarian buildings. It's a moot point whether these children would appreciate the irony of their descendants being rehoused in more comfortable and sanitary conditions, albeit miles away (*ML*), while their former home ground is occupied by Strathclyde Regional Council (*CP*).

Childcare facilities were already in place in the 1920s, which allowed women to take much-needed work. Here, a mother is being interviewed for a child's place at Cowcaddens Day Nursery in 1922. (*ML*)

Nutrition was high on the social agenda. Here, mothers and infants are waiting to be examined by Dr Sutherland at the Corporation Infant Milk Depot, 106 Maitland Street, in 1911. (*ML*)

Comparison with Maitland Street today (see pages 42–3) shows how much Cowcaddens has changed. This exterior view shows the socialist female medical pioneers Dr Sutherland and Miss McKenzie in the doorway of the Infant Milk Depot. (*ML*)

At the day nurseries, children could be assured of decent food; these are the Mount Blow children being fed and enjoying the sunshine in June 1922. (*ML*)

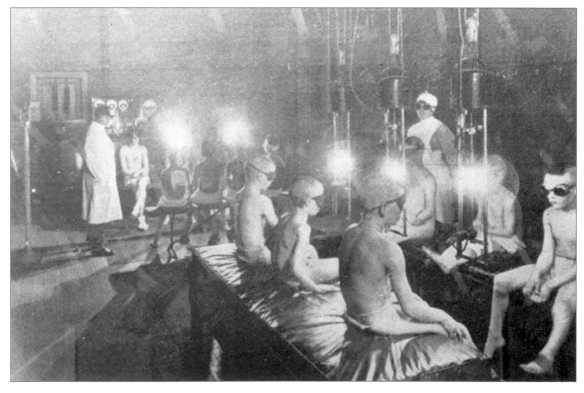

For those children who received little natural sunlight to strengthen their bones, there was always artificial light treatment, as here at Robroyston Hospital in about 1922. (*ML*)

For those who could and did play outside, there were often playground attendants to watch them. This is 'Old Bob', who looked after the playground in Bain Square, Calton, pictured in about 1900 with some of his charges (*ML*). Today, solitary skateboarding in unsupervised parks is more the norm (*CP*).

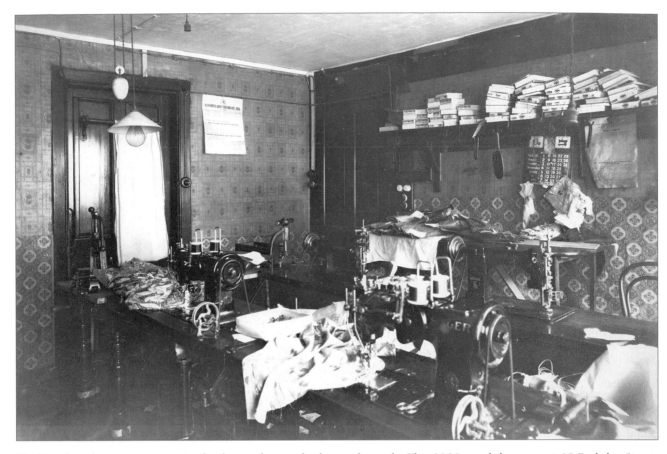

Working from home was an option for dressmakers and other craftspeople. This 1930s workshop was at 68 Berkeley Street, Anderston (*ML*). Now, the same address is an office, with a symbol of the new century's obvious prosperity parked outside (*CP*).

The feeing market at Graham Square was what passed for an employment exchange in the years before the First World War. (*ML*)

Many women found war work during the First World War. These women are making grenades at the Elmbank Foundry, Possil Road, in 1916. (*ML*)

People who had worked all their lives and reached centenarian status had the consolation of a congratulatory letter from the monarch. Mrs Mann received hers on her birthday in 1917, in her home at 81 Rottenrow. (*ML*)

Glasgow has had its share of pioneers. At the City Hall at 96 Candleriggs there is a plaque to the socialist pioneer John Maclean (1879–1923), who spoke to the crowds in this building in the early days of 'red Clydeside'. Imprisoned for a year in 1921, he declared during his defence that Glasgow was the only city in the world where the unemployed were organised and not rioting. (*CP*)

Glaswegians who fought against fascism in Spain in the 1930s have their memorial in the statue at Custom House Quay (*CP*). The inscription reads: 'Better to die on your feet than to live on your knees.'

Loyal fans heading to see Partick Thistle at Firhill, 12 April 1958. Many of them would now rather watch Serie A matches via satellite than stand on the terraces every Saturday. (*ML*)

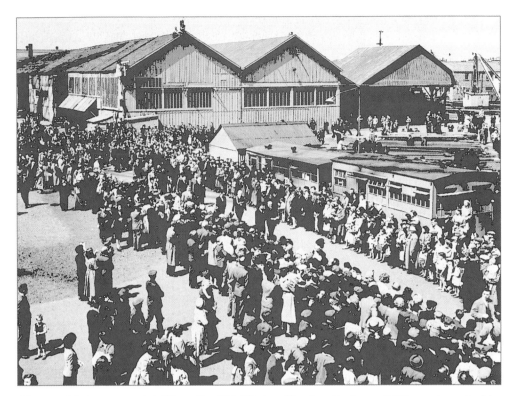

Glasgow fair loves a party! When the MV *Windsor* (Barclay, Curle no. 727) was launched by the Princess Royal during her visit to Glasgow in 1952, huge crowds turned out to see 'The Young Couple', as they were affectionately called. (*ML*)

Boats loomed large in other leisure pursuits. Here, the staff of the South of Scotland Electricity Board enjoy an outing on board the paddle-steamer *Duchess of Hamilton* in 1958. (*ML*)

The retail experience has changed markedly. This street scene on a Saturday in 1955 (*ML*) is very different from shopping in today's Sauchiehall Street. There isn't the same opportunity to congregate around barrows but at least there's a place to sit! (*CP*)

Glasgow's new-found reputation as a shopping centre second to none is emphasised by the developments in St Enoch Square, Princes Square and the Buchanan Galleries (*CP*). But if the women appreciate the benefits of retail therapy, their menfolk may not be quite so delighted at times. The child in the window probably isn't for sale (*CP*).

An example of the city's surging confidence is the stunning conversion work carried out in what is now the Italian Centre in John Street, particularly evident in the inner courtyard. (*CP*)

Perhaps the greatest bounty the twenty-first century will bring to Glasgow is that her sons will be less likely to die in some foreign field, fighting for strangers. These Royal Scots Greys, on parade in Maryhill Barracks in 1890, had the South African campaign and the 'war to end all wars' in front of them. (*ML*)

The People's Palace is virtually unchanged from 1905 when this postcard was printed (*BD*). The people of Glasgow also show the same resilience, humour in the face of adversity and all-round good sense that they always have done. If this book reminds a few of them what it used to be like and tells a few more how it is now, it will have done its job. Thank you, Glasgow – it was a blast!

Acknowledgements & Picture Credits

All the postcards reproduced in this book are from Bruce Durie's private collection, unless indicated otherwise, and the new photographs have been specially taken by Carrie Parkinson. These photographs have now been deposited with the Mitchell Library, Glasgow, as a small way of saying a big thank-you. Particular mention must be made of Mrs Edna Ryan of the Mitchell Library Glasgow Room and Mr Karl Magee, Archives and Special Collections Coordinator, who made this author's life much, much easier.

Caroline Parkinson worked in Glasgow from 1989 to 1992 (on Urban Aid programmes) and from 1994 to 1997 (in TV and film production). She started as a photographer's model and assistant in 1985 and studied with Ruth Stirling from 1994 onwards. Carrie is now a full-time photographer and graphic designer and lives in Dysart, Fife.

Images marked (*ML*) are reproduced by kind permission of Glasgow City Council and the Mitchell Library. Images marked (*CP*) are copyright © Caroline Parkinson and are reproduced here with her permission. All postcards used in this book, unless indicated otherwise, are from Bruce Durie's private collection.